LILY PAD POND

text and photographs by

BIANCA LAVIES

E. P. DUTTON · NEW YORK

ACKNOWLEDGMENTS

for sharing time and knowledge:

Dr. John Hellman, University of Maryland

Dr. Suzanne Batra, U.S. Department of Agriculture,
   Agricultural Research Center, Beltsville, Maryland

Dr. George Zug, National Museum of Natural History

Dr. Ronald Altig, Mississippi State University

Dr. Henry Wilbur, Duke University

Dr. William Shear, Hampton-Sydney College

for permission to let me work there:

City of Annapolis Water Plant

U.S. Department of Agriculture, Agricultural Research
   Center, Beltsville, Maryland

Many of the animals in this book are shown
larger than they occur in nature. Approximate
enlargements are given below.

bullfrog:
   on front cover   2x
   with snapping turtle   3½x
   catching dragonfly   2x
dragonfly:
   nymph   7x
   emerging adult   2x
   flying   2x
newts (playing)   2x
spider, fisher:
   eating   3x
   grooming   3x
tadpole (opposite first page of text)   5x
turtle:
   painted (poking head up)   2x
   snapping (swimming)   5x
water strider   17x
The bullfrog on the last page is life-size.

Copyright © 1989 by Bianca Lavies

All rights reserved.

Published in the United States by
E. P. Dutton, New York, N.Y.,
a division of NAL Penguin Inc.

Published simultaneously in Canada by
Fitzhenry & Whiteside Limited, Toronto

Designer: Riki Levinson

Printed in the U.S.A.   First Edition
10 9 8 7 6 5 4 3 2 1

Library of Congress Cataloging-in-Publication Data
Lavies, Bianca.
   Lily pad pond/Bianca Lavies.—1st ed.
   p.   cm.
   ISBN 0-525-44483-1
   1. Pond ecology—Juvenile literature.   I. Title.
QH541.5.P63L38   1989   88-31697
574.5'26322—dc19   CIP
                                                AC

This book is dedicated to
the toughest and kindest boss I had, for fourteen years:
Bob Gilka
Director of Photography 1963–1985,
National Geographic Society

A fat little tadpole lives among water lilies in a woodland pond.

One year ago, the tadpole
and her brothers and sisters
hatched from bullfrog eggs.
They were tiny tadpoles then.
Many were eaten by other pond animals
like the sunfish swimming below
the lily pad.

But not this tadpole.
After a year of eating pond ooze
and plant material, she is plump.
She rests on a water-lily stem.
Its leaves help hide her
from neighbors who might want to eat her.

This neighbor snapping turtle eats tadpoles,
clams, snails, and small fish.

This neighbor dragonfly
nymph eats tadpoles too.
It lives underwater for
a year, eating anything
it can catch.

Then one night it climbs
out of the water.
As it dries off,
its skin splits and
a wet creature with
crumpled wings crawls out.
Overnight its body expands
and its wings unfold.

The nymph has turned into an adult dragonfly.
By morning the dragonfly's wings
will be dry enough for it to fly away.

Newts are friendly neighbors.
They don't eat tadpoles.
They play among the lily pads.

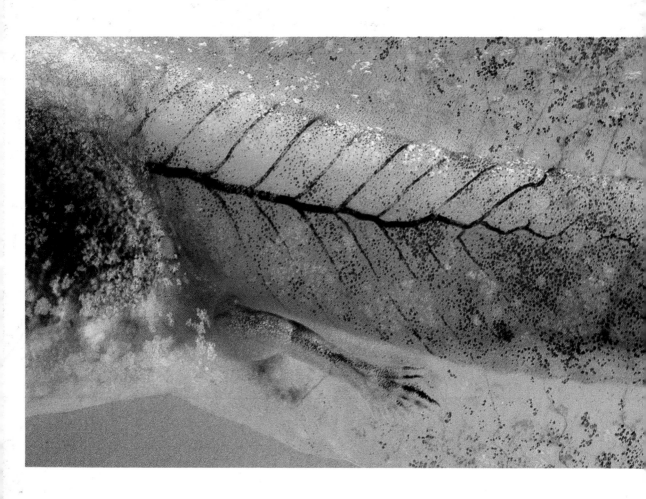

As the tadpole gets older and bigger,
her legs start to grow.
The back legs can be seen right away.
The front legs remain hidden
under a flap of skin for a while.
As they get larger, they will
push their way out, "elbows" first.
Her tail will shrink and disappear.
Then she will be...

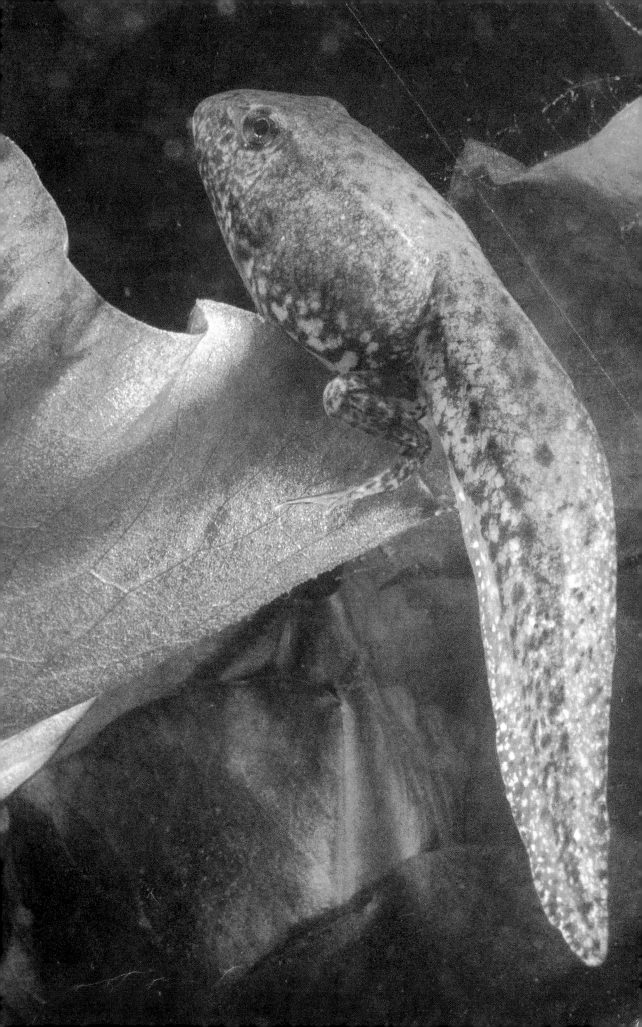

a young little bullfrog in Lily Pad Pond.
She climbs onto a log.
What else is on the log?
The snapping turtle.
The turtle won't eat her now.
She is too big.

Up pops another turtle,
a painted turtle,
looking for a place to sit.

A log is a good place for the whole family
to sunbathe.

A water strider skates
across the surface of the pond.
It has just caught an insect to eat.
With the help of hairs on the ends of its feet,
a water strider can stand on the water
without sinking.

This fisher spider has to stand on a lily pad.
If it tried to stand on the water,
down it would sink.

When the spider is startled,
it scoots under the lily pad to hide.
The many hairs on the spider's body
grow close together and repel water.
They trap air which the spider
takes underwater to breathe.
The layer of air makes the spider look silvery.

Now the fisher spider eats an insect it has caught.

Afterward, the spider grooms itself.
It cleans its eight legs
by drawing each one through its fangs.

Here comes the young little bullfrog,
looking for insects to eat—
Watch out, dragonfly!

After many more meals
over several more years,
that young little bullfrog will be—
gulp!—

a great big bullfrog in Lily Pad Pond!